LEGACIES
ARCHITECTURE

Richard Wood

Thomson Learning • New York

Legacies

Architecture
Sports and Entertainment

Cover: The ancient Pyramids at Giza, Egypt (main) and the modern pyramid outside the Louvre in Paris, France (inset). The strength and simplicity of the pyramid shape still inspire us after 5,000 years.

First published in the
United States in 1995 by
Thomson Learning
115 Fifth Avenue
New York, NY 10003

First published in Great Britain in 1994 by Wayland (Publishers) Ltd.

Library of Congress Cataloging-in-Publication Data
Wood, Richard.
  Architecture/ Richard Wood.
    p.   cm.—(Legacies)
  Includes bibliographical references (p.   ) and index.
  ISBN 1-56847-273-0
  1. Architecture, Ancient—Juvenile literature. [1. Architecture, Ancient.]
I. Title. II. Series: Legacies (New York, N.Y.).
NA210.W66   1995
722—dc20   94-32636

Printed in Italy

Contents

A legacy is something handed down from an ancestor or predecessor. The modern world has inherited many different legacies from ancient civilizations. This book explores the architectural legacies of the ancient world.

ANCIENT CIVILIZATIONS

This is where the ancient civilizations described in this book were. The approximate dates of the peak of each civilization are given under each heading. You can find the exact areas at the beginning of each civilization's chapter.

Monument Builders
c.2500 – 1000 B.C.
The massive stone circle of Stonehenge in southern England is a legacy left by the prehistoric monument builders. As they settled in communities, people built monuments all across Western Europe to honor their gods.

Ancient Celts
c.750 B.C. – A.D. 100
Celtic round houses of wattle and daub and thatched roofs were built across much of Europe as Celtic tribes spread and settled in areas they conquered.

Ancient Rome
507 B.C. – A.D. 476
The Romans developed the arch and the vault to build huge structures such as aqueducts and amphitheaters. The Colosseum amphitheater (right) was home to the Roman Games, spectacles where gladiators and wild animals fought to the death.

Ancient Greece
c.800 – 331 B.C.
Overlooking the city of Athens, the Acropolis, meaning "high city," was a sacred place with temples and shrines to the goddess Athene. Athens was a powerful city state and became the center of Greek civilization and culture in the fifth century B.C.

Ancient Middle East
Sumerians c.3500 – 2400 B.C.
Canaanites c.2500 – 1200 B.C.
Babylonians c.1900 – 539 B.C.
Phoenicians c.1200 – 146 B.C.
Hebrews c.1200 B.C. – onward
The Marsh Arabs who live in present-day Iraq still build
reed houses like those of their ancient ancestors. The
ancient Middle East was home to many ancient
civilizations, including the Sumerians, Canaanites, and
Babylonians, who built the first cities.

Ancient Asia
Mauryan dynasty, India c.322–185 B.C.
Ch'in dynasty, China c.221–206 B.C.
T'ang dynasty, China C.A.D. 618–906
Buddhist stupas, like these in Sri Lanka,
were built in the eastern civilizations of
ancient India and China, in sacred
places connected with the Buddha's life.
The stupa developed into the curved
roofed pagoda, which became the
distinctive architectural style of Asia.

Ancient Egypt
c.3100 – 30 B.C.
The ancient Egyptians built great pyramid tombs to bury their
pharaohs in. This sphinx, with a lion's body, lies outside King
Khafre's pyramid to act as guardian to his tomb.

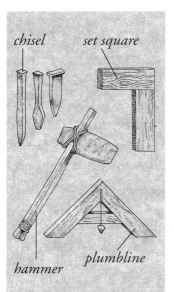

chisel   set square

hammer   plumbline

These were some of the working tools of the Egyptian pyramid builders, 4,500 years ago. A modern builder's tool kit contains some remarkably similar items.

chapter one

ARCHITECTURE:
MODERN AND ANCIENT

Architecture, unlike other art forms, comes from a primary human need – the need for shelter. Architecture can be seen in the different types and styles of buildings we see every day. Architecture affects us most in the buildings, or homes, where we and our friends and neighbors live. Homes come in many shapes and sizes. Their design depends on things such as the wealth and size of the family, their lifestyle, the country's climate, and what building materials are available nearby. These things have always affected the design of homes, ever since the earliest prehistoric peoples began to settle in family and community groups.

Some buildings are much older than others that are in the same area. Many ancient structures are now buried underground, and we have to rely on archaeologists to uncover foundations, floors, and walls of buildings buried beneath the earth. However some ancient architecture, even from prehistoric times, still exists, either as ruins or as more complete structures. A few ancient buildings are still in use 2,000 years or more after they were constructed.

◀ *The ancient city of Rome is modern Italy's capital. The Forum was an important meeting place in ancient Rome. Its ruins show its ancient architecture.*

But there is another sort of legacy, too: a legacy of ancient ideas and designs, skills, and methods. Some have come down to us through the ages by continuous use. Others were forgotten, perhaps for centuries, and then rediscovered later. The use of the plug and socket is an ancient building technique. It was how the Stone Age builders of Stonehenge, England, joined their massive stones together. The ancient Greeks used a similar method to join stone blocks to make tall columns. The Celts, in Scotland and Ireland, cut wooden joints to connect the sections of their timber-framed houses. Even today, builders often rely on this basic technique for attaching sections of buildings.

▼ *The great monuments of modern cities can be surprisingly similar to those of ancient times. Here, in Washington, DC, you can see an Egyptian-style obelisk, a Greek-style temple,and a Roman-style dome.*

▲ *Ancient builders, like modern ones, sometimes re-used designs and materials from older buildings. The Roman Emperor Constantine took pieces from buildings all over Rome to construct this arch in A.D. 315.*

Notions of beauty take us back to ancient times. In the Western world, rules about balance and proportion in design, which the Greeks first worked out almost 3,000 years ago, still influence the look of many buildings, from small houses to great public works. In Asia, traditional forms and techniques, like the curved roofs of pagodas, are still used to decorate many new buildings.

Our building materials, too, have an ancient ancestry. Choice of material still depends largely on what can be found or made locally, whether it is stone, wood, brick, or mud. Modern transportation and new inventions have widened the choice for builders today, at least in richer countries. But despite this, many ancient techniques, like the thatching and tiling of roofs, are still widely used.

Other traditional skills, like timber framing, have been adapted for modern buildings. Bricks and concrete, two of the most widely used materials of all, have been in use ever since their invention in ancient times.

The legacy of ancient architecture may be in your street or in your town. Many buildings, even new ones, can give clues about their ancestry. Look for rectangular windows, pillars, and pediments (from Greece), arches, domes, and curved roof tiles (from Rome), timbers that slot together (from Stone Age and Celtic times), and curved shapes (from Asia). See how much we still rely on bricks (introduced in the ancient Middle East) and concrete (a Roman invention). You may be surprised at how great the legacy of ancient architecture is.

▲ A piece of ancient Egypt in the heart of a modern city. Cleopatra's Needle was taken to England in the nineteenth century and stands on the bank of the Thames River in London. The Needle began a fashion for modern monuments in this shape, which is called an obelisk.

▼ *The architect Edwin Lutyens designed this World War I memorial at Thiepval, France, to remind people of a Roman triumphal arch.*

chapter two

MONUMENT BUILDERS

Monuments are objects set up to celebrate or remember things. We rarely have to travel far in the modern world to find monuments. Sometimes they are quite small, like gravestones or statues. They remind future generations of the life of one person. Sometimes they are bigger, like war memorials, designed to remind us of many people or important events. Great cities often have huge monuments that have become landmarks known all over the world, like the Eiffel Tower in Paris and the Statue of Liberty at the entrance to New York harbor. These monuments remind us of the pride people felt in their achievements and freedoms.

▲ *Every gravestone in the Arlington National Cemetery in Virginia is a monument to the life of a human being.*

The urge to build monuments is something shared by most peoples worldwide since prehistoric times. The earliest monuments of all are among the best-known structures that have ever been built by human beings.

Prehistoric monuments are all over the world. In Europe alone there are about 50,000 separate monuments. The building skills and designs seem to have arrived with the first farmers from the Middle East, after 6000 B.C. As people relied less on hunting and gathering for food, they settled in communities. They learned how to build fixed homes to live in, and often built monuments too.

Some of these Stone Age monuments consist of passages and tombs cut into rock under earth mounds. The tombs at Hal Safliene on the Mediterranean island of Malta were made almost 5,000 years ago. They held the remains of 7,000 bodies buried underground.

KEY TO MAP

Stone circle

Stone avenue

Burial mound

EUROPE

▼ **Megaliths**
Many monuments consist of megaliths, a word meaning "big stones." At Carnac in Brittany, France, nearly 1,000 stones were set on end in long rows about 7,000 years ago. They are some of the world's oldest manufactured structures.

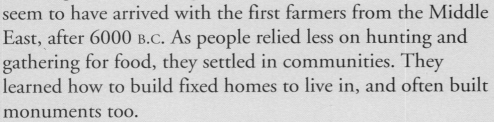

Prehistoric tombs at New Grange in Ireland lie hidden under a mound of stones and earth almost forty feet thick, surrounded by a ring of ninety-seven flat stone slabs. For a few days each winter, New Grange reveals its secret. As the sun rises on the shortest day of the year (known as the Winter Solstice), its rays shine straight down the long entrance passage. For a few moments, the domed ceiling of the central chamber glows with strange light and its carved patterns appear to come to life.

Stonehenge, in England, is perhaps the most famous prehistoric monument of all. It was built and rebuilt many times between about 2750 and 1500 B.C. The main sandstone blocks at Stonehenge weigh up to 40 tons each. They were quarried about 20 miles away, dragged to Stonehenge on wooden rollers, and raised into place using earth ramps and pulleys.

► *Stonehenge as it appears today. Nobody can be certain what it looked like in ancient times.*

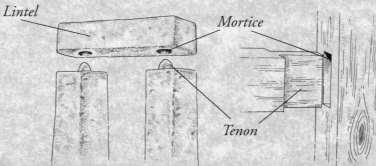

**Stonehenge:
the jigsaw puzzle**
Each huge upright stone at Stonehenge slots into the horizontal top pieces (lintels) like a plug into a socket. Builders today still use similar methods to hold sections of buildings together.

Stonehenge

Lintel

Mortice

Tenon

Modern timber joint

There are so many stones at Stonehenge that people say if you try to count them, you will never get the same number twice. Some of the smaller stones came from Wales, 150 miles away. Stonehenge's builders may have believed that the Welsh blue stone had magical qualities.

The biggest mystery of Stonehenge is why it was built at all. Was it a temple to the sun or moon, or to a snake god? Was it a palace, an assembly hall, or a cemetery? Perhaps it was an observatory for studying the stars, or a huge computer for calculating time and seasons. People once believed that Stonehenge was built by giants or fairies. Some have even said that it was built by space aliens!

▲ *Most ancient monuments are solid, but the Statue of Liberty in New York City is hollow, built around an iron skeleton. It was made in France and shipped to New York in sections in 1885.*

Greek Admiration
The Greek poet Hesiod envied the simple life of the prehistoric monument builders. He wrote: "They lived as if they were gods, their hearts were free from sorrow, and when they died it was just like falling asleep."

Crashing Walls
There is a famous
story in the Bible
which describes how
the walls of Jericho
fell when Joshua blew
his trumpet: "…and
when the army heard
the trumpet sound
they raised a great
shout, and down fell
the walls. The army
advanced on the city,
every man straight
ahead, and took it."
(Joshua 6, 20-21)

chapter three

ANCIENT
MIDDLE EAST

All over the modern world there are towns and cities where
large numbers of people live and work together. Cities provide
employment in stores, offices, and factories. They usually have
good transportation as well as
sports and entertainment. But
in ancient times, there was
another reason for building
cities – defense. People felt
safer in large numbers,
protected by strong walls,
which they built around
their cities.

The first city to be built is
believed to be Jericho, in
Jordan. The stone walls
around Jericho were built
almost 10,000 years ago,
twice as long ago as the
pyramids of Egypt. Almost as
old as Jericho was the ancient

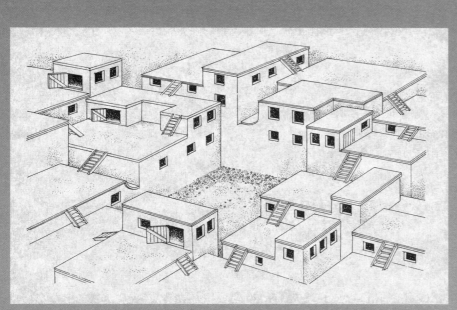

◀ **Çatal Hüyük**
The houses in Çatal Hüyük were tightly packed together, rising in terraces up the sloping hillsides. In the center of each group of buildings was an open courtyard, shared by several families.

city of Çatal Hüyük in Turkey. Archaeologists who have excavated the site of the city have found not only walls, but the remains of mud-brick homes, works of art, fragments of bone, plant pollen, and fabric. There is even a wall painting from about 6200 B.C. which shows the houses of the city with the nearby volcano Hasan Dag in the background. From their finds, archaeologists can piece together a detailed picture of everyday life in a prehistoric city.

A few thousand years later, a number of much smaller cities rose farther to the east of Turkey. These were the powerful city states of Mesopotamia, dating from about 3500 B.C., the true ancestors of modern towns and cities.

▼ The modern city of Toronto, Canada, appears to grow out of the waters of Lake Ontario. Although cities today are very different from those built 10,000 years ago, there are many similarities in how they are used.

Large cities began in Mesopotamia (modern Iraq), because this was the fertile land between the great Tigris and Euphrates rivers. By using the floods to water their rich soil, one family could grow enough food to feed many other people. Since these other people did not need to farm for them-selves, they were free to group together and form a city.

The first Mesopotamians built their houses using reeds from the river banks. There are still homes just like this in the swamps of southern Iraq. But in the cities, people soon started to use mud. Mud was strengthened with chopped straw, formed into brick shapes, then left in the hot sun to set hard. Roofs were made from palm logs and leaves. The outer walls of these houses were solid, aside from one doorway. Windows looked inward onto a shaded central courtyard. Only the larger homes of rich families were two stories high. These houses had wooden balconies along the upper floors, just like the verandas on houses in warm countries today.

▼ *The Marsh Arabs of southern Iraq today still build their homes from bundles of reeds. This simple but effective method has changed little since ancient times.*

Ancient Skyscrapers
Ziggurats were stepped brick platforms with religious temples perched on the top. The ziggurat at Ur, in modern day Iraq, stood over 250 feet high and was built in about 2100 B.C. It was made mainly of mud bricks, but with fired bricks on the outside for strength. Some 3,000 years later, the Maya people of Central America built their stone temples in the same shape. The tops of some modern New York skyscrapers have also copied this design.

Almost half of the world's population still lives in mud structures similar to those of the ancient Mesopotamians. They are cheap and easy to build, practical to live in, and they are not harmful to the environment. In some places, like Mali in West Africa, builders today are able to build sophisticated modern structures using ancient mud-building techniques. The Great Mosque at Djenne, Mali, was completed in 1907 and is the world's largest mud building. Where the Mesopotamians used to strengthen their mud walls with chopped straw, the Malians use rice and millet husks to make them more waterproof.

▲ *The Chrysler building in New York looks like a huge ancient ziggurat. When it was built in 1926 it was the world's tallest building. The wheel shapes reminded people of the cars made by the Chrysler Company.*

chapter four

ANCIENT EGYPT

The pyramids of ancient Egypt are among the wonders of the ancient world. Today, 4,800 years after they were built, they still rank alongside the greatest of human achievements. There are few designs in architecture as simple but as strong as the pyramid. With their sloping sides leading to a point, pyramids are extremely sturdy.

The pyramids had a purpose – to house the bodies of dead pharaohs (kings). The Egyptians believed that when the body died, the spirit stayed alive as long as the body was kept well and ready to receive it again. Bodies were embalmed, wrapped in cloths, and placed in a series of coffins. This process is called mummification.

▼ *The Pyramids of Giza were built about 2800 B.C. The Great Pyramid stands 450 feet high, and its base has sides 755 feet long, but the joins between the stones are less than a millimeter wide.*

◄ *This famous pyramid stands by the entrance to the Louvre museum in Paris. But instead of being solid, it is made of glass, so that each side reflects a different view of the sky. A second glass pyramid has recently been added – but this one perches on its tip, upside down!*

The pharaohs' tombs were hidden in pyramids along with their household goods and treasures. The Egyptians hoped that the strength of the pyramid would protect the tombs from robbers. Spells were written, carved, and chiseled on the walls to help the dead pharaoh's spirit on its way and to curse anyone who disturbed the ruler's rest.

Pyramid building – then and now

Few, if any, modern building works can match the skill and organization needed to build the pyramids. According to the Greek writer Herodotus, 100,000 men, fed on onions, worked for twenty years to build the Great Pyramid of Cheops. Even the largest construction company today would take just as long to do the same work using modern methods and machinery.

▲ *The tops of columns on buildings today are often decorated with carved leaves. This practice goes back to the Egyptians, who believed that their land had grown like a plant from the sea. The Egyptians decorated their own columns to look like plants such as the papyrus and lotus flowers.*

Nobody knows for certain why pyramids were built where they were. Tomb paintings suggest that they may have been positioned to represent a huge map of the stars, which were most important to the pharaohs.

Two narrow shafts lead out of the king's and queen's tombs in the Great Pyramid at Giza. It was thought that these were air vents. But scientists have calculated that when the pyramid was built, in about 2600 B.C., these shafts must have pointed directly at Orion (the king's star) and Sirius (the queen's star). Perhaps the Egyptians wanted to use the rays of the stars' light to carry the spirits of the dead king and queen up to the heavens.

Modern religious beliefs often influence the architecture of buildings just as Egyptian beliefs did. The peaceful interior of Buddhist temples helps people to meditate by focusing on the image of the Buddha. Muslim mosques point toward the holy city of Mecca. Christian churches are often cross-shaped to remind people that Jesus Christ died on a cross. Most churches also point east. This is a legacy of the ancient practice of making temples point toward the rising sun.

Ancient Greek visitors were amazed by the pyramids, but Egyptian temples most influenced their own buildings. The massive columns we can still see at Karnak today were carved in sections. The sections were piled on top of each other to form columns. Huge stone slabs were placed across the top to bridge the gaps, like the lintel stones at Stonehenge a thousand years earlier. These techniques, first developed by the ancient Egyptians, were perfected by the Greeks, then the Romans, and are still in use today.

The temples at Karnak, Egypt, began to be built in about 1990 B.C. and were added to over several centuries. The walls and columns are covered with pictures and hieroglyphic writing that praise the dead pharaohs.

chapter five

ANCIENT
GREECE

Many modern towns and cities in the Western world have buildings that look like ancient Greek temples. Instead of being temples to gods like Zeus or Athena, they might be important government buildings, like the White House in Washington, DC, or famous churches, like St. Peter's in Rome, Italy. They might be theaters, like the Bolshoi in Moscow, Russia, or museums, like the British Museum in London, England.

The style adapted from Greek temples is often called "classical" architecture. It was first copied by the Romans. Since then, people all over the world have copied this style of building, right down to our own times. They have used it for important public buildings,

▼ *The Acropolis in Athens, Greece, stands on a natural hill on which a level platform was constructed. The height ensured that the temples and statues could be seen from all over the city of Athens, and can still be seen today.*

but also for ordinary houses. When the Greeks developed their classical style, they were influenced by the Egyptians.

Greek traders were impressed by the temples and tombs they saw in Egypt. Back home, they gradually developed their own style of temple building, using the fine white marble of their country. The Greek buildings were in some ways quite unlike those in Egypt. That is because ancient Greece and Egypt were very different countries. In Egypt, one great king could command 100,000 men to build a single tomb. But Greece was made up of small islands and city states, each with its own ruler. Their temples were therefore built on a smaller scale.

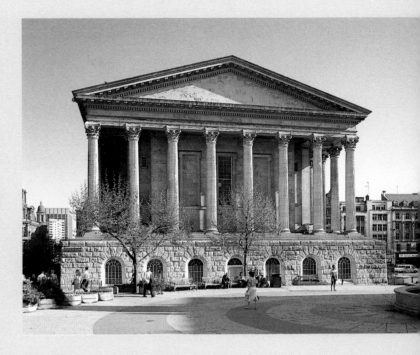

▲ *The City Hall in Birmingham, England, was designed in 1832 to look like an ancient Greek temple.*

▲ *If you look closely at the pillars of the Parthenon in Athens, Greece, you can see how precisely each stone was carved.*

The structure of Greek temples was not new. It used lines of columns to prop up the roof, with single stone blocks in between. This was no different from Egyptian, or even prehistoric buildings. What the Greeks perfected was a sense of proportion and symmetry that has never been improved to this day. They used precise mathematical rules to fix the dimensions of buildings. Having decided, for example, how wide to build a temple, the rules told them how long and high it should be, how thick to make the columns, and what gaps to leave between them.

Greek temples were built so solidly that many have survived to the present day. You can visit them not only in Greece, but also in the parts of Asia and southern Italy that were once ruled by the Greeks. The temple at Syracuse, in Sicily, was built 2,400 years ago and is still in use as a Christian church.

The strong, simple form of the Parthenon in Athens, Greece, looks best when seen against the sky from below. Its rectangular shape is misleading. All the columns are in fact tapered and tip inward so that the whole building is

◀ *The Parthenon in Athens, Greece, is perhaps the most famous temple of all. Designed in 447 B.C., it still stands on the Acropolis, a high hill overlooking the city of Athens. An exact copy of the Parthenon in Nashville, Tennesee, was constructed between 1897 and 1931.*

slightly pyramid-shaped. There are no exact right angles anywhere in the Parthenon. Nor are any two blocks of marble exactly the same, though each has a mirror image on the opposite side. Each column was made in ten or twelve pieces, then ground together to make a perfect fit and joined with plugs and sockets. So Greek temples like the Parthenon are not really the simple shapes they appear to be.

Palladio

The Italian architect Andrea Palladio (1508–80) adapted Greek rules of proportion to suit smaller buildings. Thanks to Palladio, many ordinary homes built in Europe and America owe their appearance to the ancient Greeks.

In 1769, Thomas Jefferson used Palladio's ideas to design his own house at Monticello, in Virginia. ▶

The classical style as we know it today is easy to recognize, whether or not the buildings look like temples. The style looks equally good whether it is used for a great palace like Versailles, in France, or a humble terraced house. What these have in common are perfect proportions and symmetry. The door stands exactly in the center of the front wall. An equal number of windows is placed symmetrically on either side. Windows are usually of the sash type, which slide up and down instead of having hinges. These suit the classical proportions better.

Sometimes there is a pediment (triangular shape), like the pediment at each end of a temple, over the door or under the roof. Pediments are often held up by columns, or mock columns called pilasters. Again, these are meant to add to the balanced effect and remind us of temple columns.

▼ *This is Chiswick House in London, England. It was built in 1725, and used the architect Palladio's Villa Rotunda in Italy as a model. The Villa Rotunda was built nearly 200 years earlier, in 1550.*

Very big classical-style houses often have porticos. Porticos are big pillared porches around the front door, but look almost like miniature temples in themselves. They became popular in eighteenth-century houses like Chiswick House in London, England (above), built in 1725. Their owners thought that rich people in ancient times had built porticos to show how important they were.

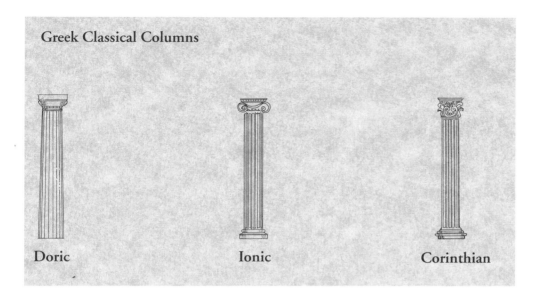

Greek Classical Columns

Doric   Ionic   Corinthian

The Greeks developed three distinct styles of column – the Doric, the Ionic, and the Corinthian. The Doric was the earliest design and had a shaft that tapered directly from the floor, appearing to grow straight out of the ground. The Doric's capital (top) was plain. The Ionic and Corinthian styles are more elegant, slender in relation to their height and crowned with graceful capitals that look like scrolls or leaves.

Inside modern homes there are machines, technology, conveniences, and comforts that the Greeks could not even dream of 2,500 years ago. But on the outside, modern houses with classical architecture have a balanced design, with the shapes of windows, doors, and other features still based on those of ancient Greek temples.

Modern domestic houses such as this one are quite small. However, classical features like pillars and pediments give them an appearance of grandeur.

chapter six

ANCIENT ROME

In ancient times, visitors to the Greek lands of the eastern Mediterranean were impressed by the beauty of Greek temples and public buildings. The Romans, in particular, developed the classical style in striking new ways. As their powerful empire expanded from North Africa to the borders of Scotland, the Romans spread their skills in design, technology, and organization.

The legacy of the Romans is all over Europe and beyond. There is Hadrian's Wall, a massive defensive barrier built all the way across northern England in A.D. 122. Roman public

▼ *The Pont du Gard, an aqueduct, was built in A.D. 14. It once carried water to the Roman city of Nimes in southern France. Its huge stone arches were a triumph of Roman engineering skill.*

buildings can still be seen, like the Porta Nigra in Trier, Germany, or the Pont du Gard bridge in France. Italy, and the city of Rome itself, probably contains the greatest number of Roman buildings.

Many roads across Europe today use the same routes that Roman surveyors and road builders first mapped out 2,000 years ago. Many European towns and cities were founded in Roman times and have been lived in ever since.

▲ At Pompeii in southern Italy you can still walk down a Roman street and step into Roman houses like the one above. They have been preserved by lava and ash, which covered the city when the nearby volcano Vesuvius erupted in A.D. 79. This "cubiculum" (bedroom), with its highly decorated walls and mosaic floor, obviously belonged to a wealthy Roman.

▼ Roman soldiers built Hadrian's Wall, England, in A.D. 122. Forts and lookout posts were placed at regular intervals to help defend against attacks from the north.

Roman architecture was more practical than Greek architecture. For a long time the Romans used Greek ideas of beauty to decorate their buildings. But the Romans were more interested in power, so they wanted to build the strongest structures for their buildings. Some of the Romans' finest work was in building aqueducts, bridges, or similar practical structures.

Rome and its empire had a much greater population than Greece. Most Romans preferred to live in towns and cities rather than the countryside. The splendid architecture of their great cities reminded the people they conquered, such as the Celts of northern Europe, that it would be dangerous to offend their Roman rulers.

Centuries later, when the British founded an even larger empire, they used architecture in a similar way, to impose their authority on the people they ruled. In this way, the buildings the British erected in India, part of their empire, owe more to Roman styles than to traditional Indian ideas.

▲ *Fort St. George looks similiar to public buildings from ancient Rome. In fact, it was built by the British in the Indian city of Madras, when India was part of the British Empire, 1,500 years after the end of the Roman Empire.*

Roman buildings sometimes looked less refined and delicate than those of the Greeks, but they were very strong. Many Roman public buildings were far too big to be constructed with post and lintel methods. Slender Grecian columns were, and still are, popular as decoration, but they were not strong enough to support the great weight of larger Roman constructions. Nor could they be used to span the much greater widths needed for huge halls and bridges. Instead the Romans turned to the arch.

A truthful builder
The Roman bridge at Alcantra, Spain, has the inscription "Pontem perfeci mansurum in saecula" (I have built a bridge to last for centuries). This is certainly true – it was built in A.D. 105 and is still in use.

31

The arch is a very simple device. It allows builders to use small stone blocks or even bricks to cross gaps that would be too long to span by other means.

This simple technique enabled the Romans to build tremendous bridges and aqueducts, many of which are still standing. Similar methods are in use to this day, but they have now been adapted for building with materials such as iron, steel, and concrete.

▲ **Building an arch**
Builders in Moscow, Russia, recently built an arch using the same techniques as the Romans developed, nearly 2,000 years ago. First, a lightweight wooden frame is built in the shape of the arch. This is used as a temporary support while the bricks or stones are fixed in place. Once the final "keystone" is in place at the top, the support can be taken away and the arch supports itself.

The Romans' next step was to develop simple arches into vaults and domes. These enabled Roman builders to hold up roofs over great spaces without the need for hundreds of columns taking up floor space. The simplest vault was like a tunnel of arches built in a line. The passages inside Roman amphitheaters, like the Colosseum in Rome, were usually made like this. It is very strong, although the walls have to be extremely thick to prevent them from being pushed outward by the weight of the vaults above.

To solve this problem, the Romans developed cross vaults. These helped to direct the forces straight down the walls rather than outward. In turn, this meant that walls could become thinner and contain large open arches or windows. This was the method used by the builders of the Baths of Diocletian in Rome. The method was so strong that you can still see the Baths as they stand today, now used as a church.

◄ *These modern vacation houses in Ibiza, Spain, show Romanesque arches of Moorish architecture. The Moors, who ruled North Africa and Spain after the Romans, inherited the Roman style of arch and we can still see its influence today.*

Long after the end of the Roman Empire, builders continued to use these methods to erect the great churches and cathedrals of medieval and modern times. Those with round (rather than pointed) arches are still called Romanesque, which reminds us of our debt to the Roman inventors of these methods.

▼ *The Colosseum in Rome was built in A.D. 71–80. It seated up to 50,000 people watching gladiators and wild animals fight to the death. The outer walls were 164 feet high, with three rows of vaulted corridors running around the edge and inward. These gave easy access to all areas of seating.*

▲ *The huge "eye" at the top of the Pantheon's dome reminded the Romans of the sun at the center of the universe.*

Roman concrete

In the third century B.C., Roman builders first discovered how to make concrete by mixing together volcanic ash, lime, sand, gravel and water. The mixture dried to become a sort of artificial rock. This was waterproof and solid, and could be set into any shape. The Romans poured it into brick compartments. Their method was the strongest until steel rods were developed in the nineteenth century.

Domes were another idea developed by the Romans from the arch and vault. Domes are really just circles of arches that all meet in the middle. The largest dome built by the Romans is the Pantheon in Rome, built about A.D. 120 as a temple for all the gods. At the very top there is a circular hole which lets light into the vast space below. From the ground the hole looks small, but it is big enough for a bus to go through. To reduce weight, the walls are hollow and get thinner higher up. The dome has a thin outer layer built on a skeleton of strong ribs. This great engineering achievement has been copied right down to the present day — a good example is the huge domed cathedral built by "Emperor" Bokhassa in central Africa in the 1980s.

The Colosseum and Pantheon, like many Roman buildings, would never have been possible without another great invention – concrete. Concrete was used to fill the 40-foot deep foundations of the Colosseum. Most of its walls and vaults were also solid concrete, with bricks on the surface. The rings of the Pantheon's dome are also made of concrete.

Concrete is not a pretty material so the Romans improved its appearance by covering its surface with bricks, marble, or mosaic patterns. Modern concrete buildings are often covered in the same way. Sydney Opera House, built in 1959–73, is made of arched concrete shells covered with white ceramic tiles. Today, concrete is still used much as the Romans used it, but it is strengthened with steel rods.

▲ *The Capitol building in Washington, DC, shows how a dome makes a building stand out and look important. This dome was added in 1851, sixty years after the main building was begun.*

▶ *Sydney Opera House in Australia is one of the world's most famous modern buildings. But its strength and shape depend on the ancient Roman inventions of concrete and arched vaulting.*

► St. Clement's temple in Rome is an early Christian church. Its design copied a Roman meeting place or basilica (below). You can see the apse at the end and the columns down the sides, which separate the side compartments.

▼ Plan of a typical Roman basilica.

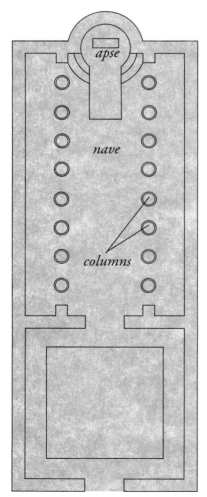

apse

nave

columns

Just as most of today's religions, such as Judaism, Hinduism, Buddhism, and Christianity, began in ancient times, so did the design of religious buildings. However, for the Christian religion, Roman temples were not suitable models because inside, there was only a small room or shrine containing the god's statue. Christian worship needed more space because Christian ceremonies took place inside a building. So instead of temples, Roman assembly halls, called basilicas, provided a better model for Christian churches. The traditional basilica was an oblong shape. It had narrow compartments down the sides, separated from the main hall by columns, like a covered arcade of stores. At the far end was a raised semicircular section called an apse, where the officials sat.

The Roman basilica was an ideal shape for Christian worship. The church altar was placed in the apse, reserved for the officials, or priests. People gathered in the main body of the basilica, now called the nave, just as the Romans had done for other sorts of meetings.

The legacy of ancient Rome has affected small houses as well as big public buildings. The beautiful houses of wealthy Romans, with their mosaic floors, open courtyards, scented formal gardens, and efficient plumbing and heating systems, have provided a model for gracious living ever since. Less wealthy Romans, however, lived in cheaply built blocks of apartments up to six stories high. In modern cities, lack of space has required similar apartment blocks, designed to house many people in a small area.

▲ This fresco, from a villa in Pompeii, shows a Roman street crowded with houses.

◀ The houses of wealthy Romans usually had a central courtyard. This one, in a house in Herculaneum, Italy, is also an open-air dining room. A mosaic plaque decorates one wall. The mosaic represents the sea-god Neptune and Amphitrite, his wife.

chapter seven

ANCIENT CELTS

The cool, moist climate of northern Europe provides ideal conditions for trees to grow. Since ancient times, the temperate zones of Europe, North America, China, Japan, and Southeast Asia, have been the home of wood-building traditions.

Modern timber-framed houses often use treated softwoods like fir or spruce, but hardwoods like oak make an even stronger building material. Oak is easy to cut when green, but dries out to an iron-like toughness. This was the wood preferred by the Celts of northern Europe 3,000 years ago.

▲ *This cottage in Normandy, France, uses timber framing and reed thatch in much the same way the Celts did 2,000 years ago.*

The Roman writer Strabo described the houses of the Celts: "Their houses are large and circular, built of planks and wickerwork, the roof being a dome of heavy thatch."

The building methods of the Celts were used over the centuries, almost until our own times. Perhaps the only reason why they are no longer widely practiced is that since about A.D. 1700, trees have been in short supply and bricks have become cheaper.

From archaeological remains we know enough about Celtic wooden buildings to be able to reconstruct them very accurately. One reason the originals no longer survive is that they were constructed around wooden posts set directly into the ground. Over time, these posts have rotted away, leaving only marks in the soil where they once stood.

Later wooden houses, from about A.D. 1300 onward, were usually built on low brick or stone walls. These gave better protection from the damp earth, and many such buildings still exist for us to see. The steep straw or reed-thatched roofs of these later houses were also built using Celtic methods. Thatched roofs are still in use today in many parts of the world.

▲ The Akha tribe in Thailand, like the Celts 2,000 years ago, have made use of the most easily available material to build their houses – trees from the natural forest of northern Thailand.

▼ These buildings at Butser, England, are modern models of ancient Celtic round houses.

Wattle and daub
The Celts filled the gaps between their upright timbers with woven panels of sticks (wattles). Onto these they splattered a mixture of mud, clay, straw, and cow dung (daub) which hardened as it dried.

chapter eight

ANCIENT ASIA

Just as Christian church architecture is still based on ancient models, in Asia the design of modern temples, such as the Lakshmi Nerain in New Delhi, is based on the ancient traditions of the Hindu and Buddhist faiths.

By 1500 B.C., many people in India were already living in cities. These were often far larger than those in Mesopotamia, with carefully planned streets of two-story houses, built of kiln-fired bricks. Curiously, their early temples were made of wood rather

▲ *These Buddhist stupas in Anuradhapura, the ancient capital of Sri Lanka, are over 2,000 years old. They are built of sun-dried mud bricks and painted white to reflect the sun.*

than brick. However, with the spread of Buddhism from the fifth century B.C. onward, temples were often built of brick or stone. Their design exactly copied that of the earlier wooden structures, right down to imitating the shape of their wooden beams.

The Buddhist stupa was originally a simple dome, built to house the remains of the Buddha and his followers. Soon stupas were extended upward. Their tall towers had many stories, each with a separate, umbrella-shaped roof. These towers were meant to represent the axis (line) on which the world turned. The stupa at Peshawur was over 650 feet high, and topped with twenty-five rows of copper umbrellas.

Buddhism was the religion of merchants who traded far across the mountains of Tibet into China. Wherever they went, they took their religion and its distinctive architecture. In China and Japan, the Buddhist stupa soon developed into the distinctive oriental style of the pagoda. Pagodas, with their great curved roofs overhanging the walls, in turn influenced the design of other buildings.

▲ Pagoda-shaped buildings are all over the world today. Many cities like Sydney, Australia (above) and New York have a Chinatown area where communities of Chinese people live. They decorate some of their buildings in the traditional oriental styles which date back to ancient times.

▼ The skyline of this modern temple in Delhi, India, is based on architectural ideas going back almost 2,500 years.

▼ *Perhaps the most remarkable of all ancient Chinese buildings was not a temple but a wall. The Great Wall of China was completed by the Emperor Ch'in Shih Huang Ti in 215 B.C. He was the first ruler of all China, and built the wall to protect his country against nomadic tribes from the north. The wall stretches for 1,400 miles across northern China. It varies in height between 18 and 30 feet, and has 25,000 watch towers at regular intervals. It is the only work of architecture that can be seen from outer space.*

In the great cities of Asia today, builders usually prefer the Western style of skyscrapers and apartment blocks. But you can still find many reminders of ancient styles in older buildings, and local architects often try to combine traditional and modern methods.

It was not until the fifteenth century that Europeans first set eyes on the wonders of the Far East. They were amazed by the beauty of oriental silk clothing and shiny glazed pottery (still called "china"), as well as the elegant Asian houses and temples with distinctively curved roofs. Ideas and illustrations began to filter through, along with goods like silks, spices, and an herbal drink called tea.

By the 1700s, oriental goods and styles were fashionable among wealthy people across Europe. No country mansion was complete without its "chinoiserie" room, with oriental-style wallpaper, furniture, and decorations. Sometimes the fashion even spread to the buildings themselves, such as at the Royal Pavilion in Brighton, England. Here, in the early 1800s, the Prince Regent extended his seaside house with an amazing mixture of styles from India, China, and Japan.

▲ *Even the chimneys of Brighton's Royal Pavilion, in England, are designed to look like the towers of an Indian temple.*

Northern Europe

Before 3000 B.C.	2000 B.C.	1000 B.C.	0	A.D.

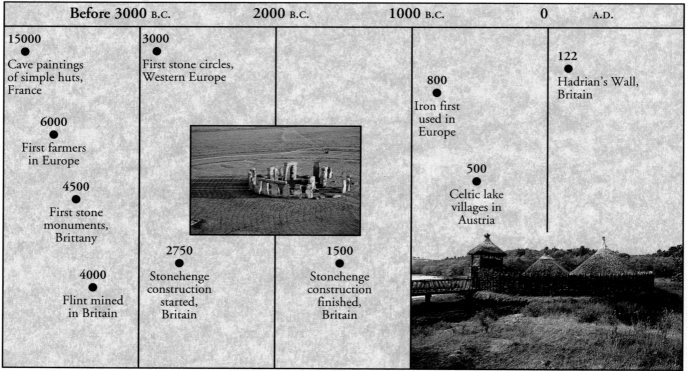

15000
Cave paintings
of simple huts,
France

6000
First farmers
in Europe

4500
First stone
monuments,
Brittany

4000
Flint mined
in Britain

3000
First stone circles,
Western Europe

2750
Stonehenge
construction
started,
Britain

1500
Stonehenge
construction
finished,
Britain

800
Iron first
used in
Europe

500
Celtic lake
villages in
Austria

122
Hadrian's Wall,
Britain

Far East and Americas

Before 3000 B.C.	2000 B.C.	1000 B.C.	0	A.D

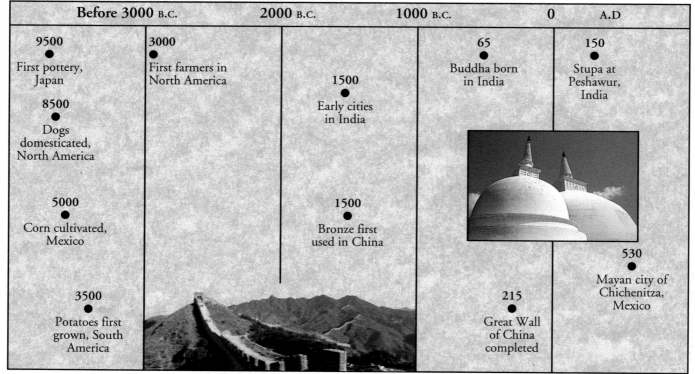

9500
First pottery,
Japan

8500
Dogs
domesticated,
North America

5000
Corn cultivated,
Mexico

3500
Potatoes first
grown, South
America

3000
First farmers in
North America

1500
Early cities
in India

1500
Bronze first
used in China

65
Buddha born
in India

215
Great Wall
of China
completed

150
Stupa at
Peshawur,
India

530
Mayan city of
Chichenitza,
Mexico

The Middle East

Before 3000 B.C.		2000 B.C.	1000 B.C.	0 A.D.

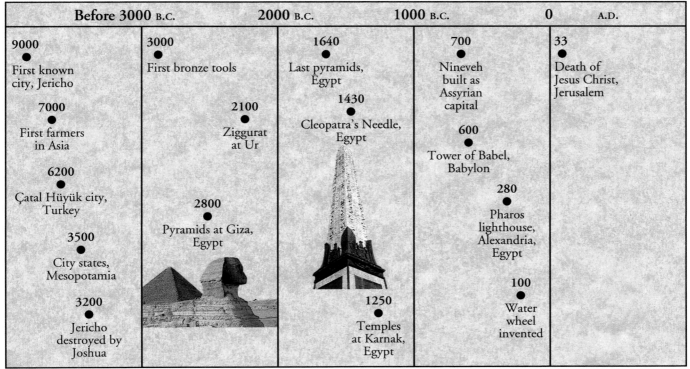

9000
First known city, Jericho

7000
First farmers in Asia

6200
Çatal Hüyük city, Turkey

3500
City states, Mesopotamia

3200
Jericho destroyed by Joshua

3000
First bronze tools

2100
Ziggurat at Ur

2800
Pyramids at Giza, Egypt

1640
Last pyramids, Egypt

1430
Cleopatra's Needle, Egypt

1250
Temples at Karnak, Egypt

700
Nineveh built as Assyrian capital

600
Tower of Babel, Babylon

280
Pharos lighthouse, Alexandria, Egypt

100
Water wheel invented

33
Death of Jesus Christ, Jerusalem

The Mediterranean Lands

Before 3000 B.C.		2000 B.C.	1000 B.C.	0 A.D.

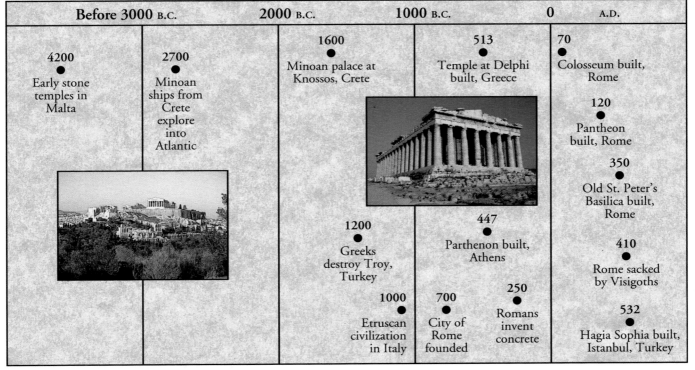

4200
Early stone temples in Malta

2700
Minoan ships from Crete explore into Atlantic

1600
Minoan palace at Knossos, Crete

1200
Greeks destroy Troy, Turkey

1000
Etruscan civilization in Italy

513
Temple at Delphi built, Greece

447
Parthenon built, Athens

700
City of Rome founded

250
Romans invent concrete

70
Colosseum built, Rome

120
Pantheon built, Rome

350
Old St. Peter's Basilica built, Rome

410
Rome sacked by Visigoths

532
Hagia Sophia built, Istanbul, Turkey

GLOSSARY

Aqueducts   Bridges for carrying water above ground.

Amphitheaters   Circular or oval meeting places for performances.

Apse   A rounded end to a rectangular building.

Archaeologists   People who study ancient remains.

Balconies   Raised platforms attached to the wall of a building.

Basilicas   Oblong meeting halls.

Buddha   The founder of Buddhism who lived in about 563–483 B.C.

Chinoiserie   Chinese style.

Domestic   To do with homes and families.

Embalmed   Preserved from decay with special fluids.

Fertile   Fruitful, or good for growing crops.

Fragments   Small pieces, often broken off a larger object.

Megaliths   Large stones used as monuments.

Mummified   Having been dried for preservation.

Nave   The main body of a church building.

Observatory   A place for studying the sky and stars.

Oriental   From Asia.

Pagodas   Tall towers with many roofs at different levels.

Pediments   Triangular roof shapes over doors, windows, or pillars.

Pilasters   Decorations that look like pillars.

Pollen   A dusty substance that plants use for fertilization.

Prehistoric   From the earliest times before written records.

Proportion   How sizes and shapes relate to each other.

Romanesque   Roman-style of architecture.

Solstice   Times of the year when the sun is farthest north or farthest south of the equator.

Sophisticated   Carefully planned, or complicated.

Stupa   A dome-shaped temple building.

Symmetry   Equality on both sides of a dividing line.

Tapered   Narrowing toward one end.

Temperate zones   Regions that are never very hot or very cold, where trees grow well.

Vaults   Arch-shaped ceilings.

Vents   Openings that permit the flow of air.

Ziggurats   Stepped towers.

FURTHER READING

Coote, Roger. *Roman Cities*. Beginning History. New York: Bookwright Press, 1990.

Dunn, Andrew. *Skyscrapers*. Structures. New York: Thomson Learning, 1993.

Macaulay, David. *Pyramid*. Boston: Houghton Mifflin, 1975.

Millard, Anne. *The Atlas of the Ancient World*. New York: Dorling Kindersley, 1994.

Millea, Nicholas. *Settlements*. Young Geographer. New York: Thomson Learning, 1993.

Oliphant, Margaret. *Earliest Civilizations*. New York: Facts on File, 1993.

Smith, Bert. *Castles*. First Books. New York: Franklin Watts, 1988.

Wood, Richard. *The Builder Through History*. Journey Through History. New York: Thomson Learning, 1994.

Picture acknowledgments:
The publishers would like to thank the following for allowing their pictures to be used in this book:
Ancient Art & Architecture Collection 9, 28-29; Eye Ubiquitous 5 (top right), 20, 25 (top), 36, 38, 40, 44 (bottom right), 45 (bottom right); Robert Harding 5 (top left), 6, 8, 9, 16, 25 (bottom), 31, 33 (top), 39 (top), 45 (top right); Images Colour Library 42-43, 44; Tony Stone Worldwide *Cover (main),* 4 (top, second & third down), 7, 10 (top), 10-11, 12-13, 13 (top), 14-15, 18-19, 21, 22-23, 23 (top), 26, 27, 30, 33, 34, 35 (top & bottom), 40-41, 43 (top); Werner Forman Archive 4 (top), 24, 29, 37 (top & bottom), 38-39, 44 (top right); Richard Wood 32; Wayland Picture Library 4 (bottom), 5 (bottom), 45 (top left & bottom left); Zefa *Cover (inset),* 17, 19 (top), 44 (top left).
All artwork is by Peter Bull.

INDEX

Numbers in **bold** refer to illustrations.